The Secrets of Animals

A CHAPTER BOOK

By Ann O. Squire

children's press®

A Division of Scholastic Inc.
New York   Toronto   London   Auckland   Sydney
Mexico City   New Delhi   Hong Kong
Danbury, Connecticut

For Evan and Emma

ACKNOWLEDGMENTS

The author and publisher would like to thank all those who gave their time and knowledge to help with this book. In particular, special thanks go to Tierney Thys, Marine Biologist, Sea Studios Foundation, Monterey, California; Scott Davis, Great White Adventures; and Luke Dollar, Doctoral Student, School of Environment and Earth Sciences, Duke University.

Library of Congress Cataloging-in-Publication Data

Squire, Ann.
 The secret lives of animals: a chapter book / by Ann O. Squire.
   p. cm. — (True tales)
 Includes bibliographical references and index.
   ISBN 0-516-25189-9 (lib. bdg.)   0-516-25457-X (pbk.)
 1. Animals—Research—Juvenile literature. I. Title. II. Series.

QL51.S75 2005
590—dc22
                                        2005004780

© 2005 Nancy Hall, Inc.
Published in 2005 by Children's Press, an imprint of Scholastic Library Publishing.
All rights reserved. Published simultaneously in Canada.
Printed in China.

CHILDREN'S PRESS and associated logos are trademarks and or registered trademarks of Scholastic Library Publishing. SCHOLASTIC and associated logos are trademarks and or registered trademarks of Scholastic Inc.

CONTENTS

Introduction	5
Chapter One Secrets of the Sunfish	6
Chapter Two Spying on Sharks	16
Chapter Three Monkey Business	24
Chapter Four The Mysterious Fossa	34
Glossary	44
Find Out More	46
Index	47

INTRODUCTION

People and animals have shared the Earth for millions of years. Some of these animals, such as dogs and cats, are almost like members of our families. We know a great deal about certain wild animals, as well.

Many other animals remain a mystery. The giant ocean sunfish and the great white shark both live in the ocean. It is difficult to find them and observe their behavior.

Even animals that live on dry land are sometimes hard to spot. The mandrill, a **primate** that lives in the rain forest, is very shy. One of the world's strangest animals lives on the island of **Madagascar**. The fossa looks like a cross between a dog and a cat. It is so mysterious that, until recently, no one had ever been able to photograph it.

Scientists are coming up with new ways of studying these hard-to-find creatures. In this book, you will meet four researchers. Their jobs are to investigate the secret lives of animals.

CHAPTER ONE

SECRETS OF THE SUNFISH

Imagine a fish shaped like a giant lima bean. Its body seems to be part of its head. It has two huge shark like fins. This fish, which can grow to be 11 feet (3 meters) long and weigh up to 5,000 pounds (2,268 kilograms), is the mysterious ocean sunfish. The sunfish gets its name partly from its round shape. It also has the habit of lying sideways on the ocean's surface, looking as if it is sunbathing. Other names for this fish include mola, moon fish, swimming head, and toppled car fish.

Ocean sunfish

The ocean sunfish has an unusual shape.

Jellyfish

Ocean sunfish live along the coastlines of many of the world's oceans. Though they will eat almost anything, their favorite food is jellyfish. When they hatch, ocean sunfish are very tiny. They are only about one-tenth of an inch (0.25 centimeters) long. Amazingly, these babies can grow to be some of the largest and heaviest fish in the sea. If a sunfish lives to adulthood, it can reach over 60 million times its starting weight!

Because ocean sunfish are so big, most other fish leave them alone. Some of their natural enemies are great white sharks, killer whales, and sea lions. Unfortunately, people are also responsible for the deaths of thousands of sunfish every year. When fishermen put out **drift nets** to capture swordfish, they accidentally catch many sunfish as well.

Great white shark

Killer whales

Sea lion

Drift nets ensnare many sunfish.

Even though the ocean sunfish is so large and unusual, not much is known about it. Scientists have many questions. How far do ocean sunfish travel each year? How deep do they dive? How many different kinds of sunfish are there? With so many being caught and injured each year in drift nets, will ocean sunfish soon be **endangered**?

One of the scientists working to answer these questions is Tierney Thys. Tierney was born in California. She has loved the water ever since she was a child. After graduating

Tierney Thys (right) and a fellow scientist tracking sunfish

Tierney swims behind a sunfish.

from college, she decided to devote her career to studying ocean life. While she was in graduate school, Tierney saw a picture of an ocean sunfish on her professor's wall. That was the beginning of her fascination with these unusual fish.

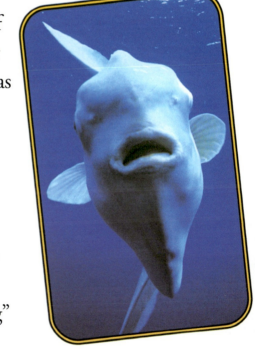

Tierney has been studying giant ocean sunfish since 2000. She has come up with a clever way of "following" these fish and studying

A satellite in space

their behaviors. She captures a sunfish and attaches a special tag to one of its fins. The tag is called a pop-up archival transmitting tag, or **PAT**. As the released sunfish moves through the water, the PAT tag records temperature, depth, and the amount of light. A few months to several years later, the tag pops out of the sunfish's fin and floats to the surface. The sunfish swims away unharmed.

Once it reaches the surface, the PAT tag begins sending its information to a **satellite** circling the Earth. The satellite sends the information to a ground station and to Tierney's computer. Tierney uses the information to pinpoint the fish's location, how far it has traveled, and how deep it dived.

Tierney and her team have tagged more than twenty ocean sunfish off the coasts of California, Australia, Japan, and South Africa. She has discovered that these fish do not travel great distances. Instead, they stick

close to home. They are, however, active divers. They make many dives to the ocean's cold depths, most probably returning to the surface to warm up.

Tierney hopes her tracking work will help her find out more about the ocean sunfish's daily behaviors and seasonal movement patterns. With this information, she may be able to help fishermen lower the number of sunfish that are accidentally caught in drift nets.

The more Tierney learns about sunfish, the more excited she is about the possibilities of ocean research. She says, "I hope all aspects of my work can help raise awareness of the oceans."

There is still much more to be learned about the ocean sunfish.

CHAPTER TWO

SPYING ON SHARKS

Scott Davis is a scientist from the Institute of Marine Sciences in California. He is using PAT tags to track the movements and behavior of the fearsome great white shark. Because of television shows and movies like *Jaws*, people think they know a lot about great white sharks. In reality, little is known about how many great whites exist, where they **breed**, how long they live, and how far they travel. What *is* known is that great white sharks

Scott Davis

Scientists are trying to learn more about great white sharks.

may be in danger of **extinction**. These sharks sometimes get caught in nets set for other kinds of fish. They are also hunted for their fins, which are considered **delicacies** in some parts of the world.

In order to save great white sharks, scientists need to find out more about them. That's where the PAT tags come in. Scott Davis is an expert scuba diver, but he knows that it's not a very good idea to get in the water with a great white shark. Instead, he goes out in a small boat. He looks for

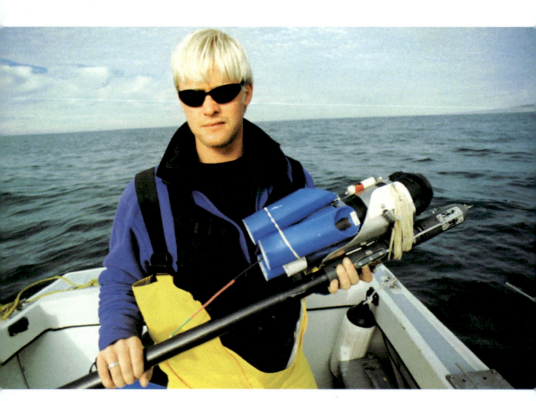

Scott in his boat

A wooden cutout of a seal attracts a shark.

sharks, which come close to shore to hunt for seals. To attract a shark, Scott places a wooden cutout of a seal into the water. When the shark gets close enough, Scott takes a photo of its fins. The photo will allow him to identify the shark in the future. Then Scott quickly and carefully attaches a PAT tag to the shark's top fin.

Although it might seem dangerous to get so close to a great white shark, Scott says that most of the sharks he meets are not **aggressive**.

Seals are a favorite meal of great white sharks.

19

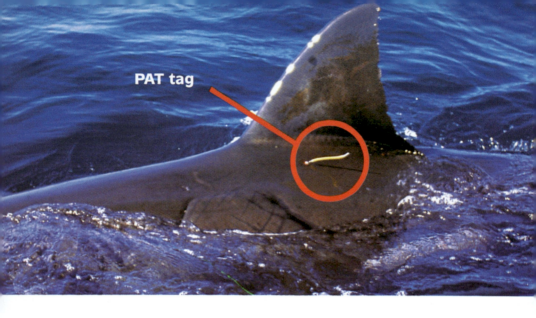

Sometimes a shark will approach the boat and try to bump against it. When that happens, Scott and his fellow scientists push the shark away with a gentle, but firm, nudge. Sometimes the researchers have to sit in their small boat for several hours, bobbing up and down in the choppy water, before a shark appears. On these days, says Scott, the greatest danger the team faces is seasickness.

Once a shark has been tagged and swims away, the PAT tag begins its job of recording water depth, temperature, and the amount of light. Each tag is programmed to come off on a certain date. Then it will pop to the surface and send its information through a satellite to Scott's laboratory computer.

Six adult white sharks were photographed and tagged off the coast of California between 1999 and 2000. When Scott looked at the data on his computer, he was surprised. Before this tagging study, scientists believed that great white sharks spent most of their time close to shore, hunting for seals and sea lions. The PAT tags showed that the sharks had traveled much farther out to sea than the scientists had expected. One of the sharks swam from California all the way to Hawaii. That's a distance of 2,800 miles (4,506 kilometers)! Other tagged sharks also

traveled long distances into the open ocean. They remained there for several months.

Scott discovered that the sharks spent most of their time either in deep water or right at the surface. He also found that they spent more time diving far out in the open ocean than he would have expected. Future tagging studies will help Scott and other researchers find out exactly what this means.

As Earth's population grows, people will turn to the oceans more and more for food and other **resources.** When this happens, great white sharks and other sea creatures will be put in danger. The first step in protecting these animals is to find out as much as possible about their movements and behavior. Scott Davis and other marine scientists believe that electronic tagging is one of the keys that will help unlock the mysteries of great white sharks and other secretive animals of the ocean.

Learning more about great white sharks will help scientists protect them.

CHAPTER THREE

MONKEY BUSINESS

With their bright red or sky-blue muzzles and blue backsides, mandrills deserve the title of "world's most colorful **mammal**." Because mandrills are so brightly colored, you would think they'd be easy to spot.

Not so, says Alan Dixson, a **zoologist** who has studied mandrills for many years. For one thing, mandrills are very shy and secretive. They move quickly, rarely stopping to rest. Also, mandrills make their homes in the rain forests of Africa. There, the trees and vines are so thick that it is nearly impossible for people

Alan Dixson

Not much is known about the shy and secretive mandrill.

to make their way through. For these reasons, the mandrill is one of Earth's least understood primates.

Alan knows how hard it can be to try to observe mandrills in the wild. "It is very difficult to see them in the forest," he says, "but when you do, the first thing you see is a flash of color through the undergrowth, a flash of nose or rump." He goes on to say that the best way for people to travel through the forest is to use paths made by elephants. The danger, of course, is that you might meet an elephant!

Alan has long been fascinated by mandrills and their social behavior. He was

Elephants make paths in the forests.

Observation towers let scientists watch animals without the animals seeing them.

especially interested in finding out why male mandrills have such bright colors. He had noticed that some males were more colorful than others. He wanted to learn whether these mandrills behaved differently from their less colorful relatives.

Alan knew that it would be nearly impossible to follow the mandrills through the forest. He solved this problem by building an observation tower near where mandrills often came to feed. After many hours of observation, he had some answers. He discovered that the males with the brightest colors were the most social. They

Brightly colored male mandrills, like the one above, are more social and more aggressive than dull-colored males.

also were the most aggressive and had mated with the most females. The more dull-colored males, on the other hand, were less aggressive and not as involved with other mandrills. They spent less time with the group. Some even lived alone.

Alan got blood samples from some of the mandrills. When he tested the blood, he found that the largest and most colorful male had fathered the most **offspring.** This male also had the highest levels of a **hormone** called **testosterone**. Not surprisingly, the dull-colored males had lower levels of this hormone, and had fathered fewer babies.

Another interesting discovery was that the dull-colored males did not always stay dull colored. If something happened to the dominant male, one of the less dominant males could sometimes take his place. When that happened, the previously dull-colored

A mother mandrill with her young

male became bright and colorful. He also became more aggressive, and his hormone levels went up.

Alan believes that less **dominant** male mandrills are able to **suppress** their hormone levels and their bright colors. Since they are not likely to find mates, why put energy into growing big and strong and colorful?

Alan did his studies of mandrills in Gabon, a small country in West Africa. Gabon is one of the least **developed** places on the African continent. Most of Gabon is still covered by rain forest. It is home to many kinds of primates, as well as forest

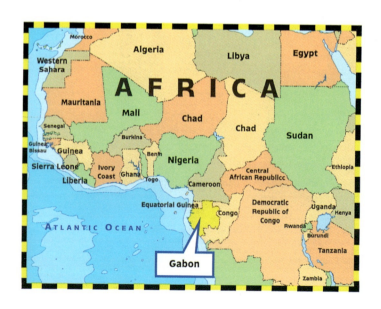

elephants, parrots, bats, snakes, and thousands of other amazing animals. The rain forest is truly a magical place.

This magic may not last forever. Alan and other scientists are worried that the rain forests are in danger. People have begun drilling for oil and mining for gold and other minerals. Logging companies are cutting down the rain-forest trees.

With rain forests being cut down, mandrills and other rain-forest animals are in danger.

A railroad has been built so that people can move around the country more easily.

All these changes threaten the mandrills and other rain-forest animals. In order to save these species, we must learn as much about them as we can. This is why research like Alan's is so important. By unlocking the mysteries of the mandrills' way of life, he and other scientists are taking the first step toward saving these animals and the forests they call home.

Scientists continue to study mandrills. What they find out might one day save the species.

CHAPTER FOUR

THE MYSTERIOUS FOSSA

On the island of Madagascar lives one of the world's strangest creatures. This meat-eating mammal looks a bit like a short, stocky mountain lion. It seems to have a leopard's sharp teeth, a dog's nose, the whiskers of an otter, and a long tail.

Scientist Luke Dollar has become an expert on fossas. He started studying them almost by accident. Luke first traveled to Madagascar in 1994. He was

Fossa

Madagascar is home to many unusual-looking creatures, including the fossa.

interested in tracking lemurs, small primates that live in the rain forest. One day, one of his lemur subjects disappeared. When Luke finally found its radio collar, all that was left were some bones and tufts of fur. Luke's guide, a native of Madagascar, was scared. He told Luke that the lemur had probably been eaten by a fierce **predator** called a fossa.

Luke was fascinated. He wanted to learn more about this mysterious animal that few scientists even knew about. The next time he returned to Madagascar, he started a project to investigate the secret life of the fossa.

Fossas live in the dense rain forest. They are very good at hiding, so the first challenge that Luke

**Luke Dollar
with a lemur**

faced was figuring out how to find them. He set up cameras and placed wire-cage traps throughout the forest. Then he waited to see if he would capture any fossas, either on film or in one of his traps.

Luke's efforts were successful. Over the years he has photographed, trapped, studied, and released many fossas. Luke and his team weigh and measure the animals and take blood samples. They attach radio collars so the animals' movements can be tracked.

Luke tagging a fossa

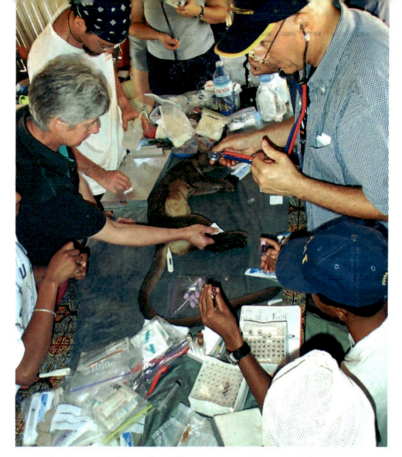

A team of scientists examines a fossa.

Luke has done **genetic** testing on the fossa. It has showed that even though the fossa looks like a cat, it is actually a close relative of the **mongoose**. It was once thought that fossas hunted only lemurs. Luke's research has shown that fossas will eat almost anything, from mice to wild pigs.

Data from the radio collars have provided more clues about the fossa. Luke has learned that fossas travel as much as

16 miles (26 kilometers) per day through the forest in search of food.

One of Luke's strangest discoveries about fossas is that their big toes are on the outside of their feet rather than on the inside. This odd arrangement, he says, helps the fossa grip tree trunks and run from branch to branch easily.

Luke began his studies of fossas mainly to learn more about these mysterious animals. These days, he is using this information to help protect fossas. They are becoming endangered in their forest **habitat.**

Fossas are endangered for several reasons. One is that many people in Madagascar are afraid of them. Fossas

A mother fossa cares for her young for more than a year.

sometimes attack chickens and other livestock. Farmers consider them pests and kill them whenever they get the chance.

Another threat to fossas is **deforestation.** The forests of Madagascar are being cut down quickly to make way for human towns or farms. In fact, today, Madagascar has less than one-tenth of its original rain forest. With their forest home disappearing, fossas are in danger of disappearing as well. Luke estimates that there are fewer than 3,000 fossas left in the undisturbed rain forests of Madagascar.

Luke with a fossa

Luke and his team are working hard to save fossas. Luke has started programs to educate the local people. His program points out that fossas can actually help people by killing the rats and wild pigs that sometimes destroy farmers' crops.

Luke is also studying the problem of deforestation. He is working with the people of Madagascar on ways to save the

As rain forests are being cut down, fossas are disappearing.

forests. One good idea is something called **ecotourism.** The local people are building bungalows and lodges in Madagascar's rain-forest parks. They hope this will attract visitors who are eager to see the country's beautiful scenery and amazing wildlife. Ecotourism will help Madagascar make money and preserve its rain forests at the same time.

Luke Dollar is hopeful that these conservation efforts will pay off, so that the fossas and their rain-forest habitat will be with us for many years to come.

Ecotourism might help save Madagascar's rain forests and fossas.

GLOSSARY

aggressive ready to threaten others or fight

breed to make offspring

deforestation the cutting down of all the trees in a forest

delicacy something rare and pleasing to eat

developed having a high level of industry

dominant in charge

drift net a huge fishing net that drifts with the tide or current

ecotourism touring natural habitats without disturbing or destroying them

endangered in danger of becoming extinct

extinction the state of no longer existing

genetic relating to genes and how traits are passed down

habitat the environment where an animal or plant naturally lives and grows

hormone a substance made by the body that effects an animal's appearance or behavior

Madagascar an island country in the Indian Ocean off the coast of Africa

mammal a warm-blooded animal that has a backbone and feeds milk to its young

mongoose a slender long-tailed mammal

offspring an animal's young

PAT (pop-up archival transmitting tag) a tag attached to sea animals that records water temperature, depth, and amount of light

predator an animal that hunts other animals

primate the order of animals that includes humans, apes, and monkeys

resource something valuable or useful

satellite a spacecraft sent out to orbit the Earth

suppress to stop from happening

testosterone a hormone found in male animals

zoologist a scientist who studies animals

FIND OUT MORE

Secrets of the Sunfish
www.oceansunfish.org
Look at photos of sunfish and read more about these mysterious sea creatures.

www.nationalgeographic.com/emerging/profiles/thys.html
Read a profile on Tierney Thys.

Spying on Sharks
www.nationalgeographic.com/kids/creature_feature/0206/sharks.html
Learn fun facts about the great white shark and watch a video of it.

Monkey Business
www.pbs.org/wnet/nature/mask/mystery.html
Read more about mandrills, Alan Dixson's research, and the country of Gabon, where mandrills make their home.

The Mysterious Fossa
http://news.nationalgeographic.com/kids/2004/07/fossa.html
Learn more about Luke Dollar and his research on fossas in Madagascar.

More Books to Read

In Search of Lemurs: My Days and Nights in a Madagascar Rain Forest by Joyce Ann Powzyk, National Geographical Society, 1998

The Truth about Great White Sharks by Mary M. Cerullo, Chronicle Books, 2000

Working with Wildlife: A Guide to Careers in the Animal World by Thane Maynard, Franklin Watts, 2000

INDEX

Africa, 24, 30, 37
Australia, 13
California, 10, 13, 16, 21
Davis, Scott, 16, 18-22
Dixson, Alan, 24, 26-28, 30, 32
Dollar, Luke, 34, 36-42
fossas, 4-5, 34-43
Gabon, West Africa, 30
great white sharks, 4-5, 16-23
Hawaii, 21
Institute of Marine Sciences, 16
Japan, 13
Jaws, 6
Madagascar, 5, 34-37, 40-43
mandrills, 4-5, 24-33
ocean sunfish, 4-15
PAT tags, 12, 18-21
rain forests, 24, 30-31, 36, 40-42
South Africa, 13
Thys, Tierney, 10-14

PHOTO CREDITS

Cover, 4 (bottom left)**, 25, 33** © Creatas/PictureQuest

1, 4 (bottom right)**, 34, 35, 36, 37, 38, 40** © Luke Dollar

3, 4 (top left)**, 6, 7, 10, 11, 15** © Mike Johnson

4 (top right)**, 16, 17, 18, 19, 20** © Scott Davis

8, 9 (middle left)**, 9** (bottom)**, 12, 31** (middle left)**, 31** (middle right) © AbleStock

9 (middle right) Courtesy of The Marine Mammal Center, Sausalito, CA

9 (top)**, 23, 26, 31** (top left) © Digital Vision/PictureQuest

24 © Courtesy of San Diego Zoo

27 © Victor R. Caivano /AP Wide World

28, 29 © Gallo Images/CORBIS

31 (bottom) © Ray Bird/Frank Lane Picture Agency/CORBIS

39 © Ken Bohn/San Diego Zoo/AP Wide World

41 © Louise Gubb/CORBIS

43 © Michael Melford/TIB /Getty Images

MEET THE AUTHOR

Ann O. Squire has a Ph.D. in animal behavior. Before becoming a writer, she spent several years studying African electric fish and the special signals they use to communicate with each other. She has also studied tropical fish in the Bahamas. Dr. Squire is the author of many books on animals and natural science topics. She lives with her children, Emma and Evan, and their cat, Isabel, in Katonah, New York.